Zen Gummies

Your Handbook for Reducing Stress

Harmony Royce

DEDICATION

May this work open doors to knowledge and opportunity for those who dream big, work persistently, and inspire without end.

CONTENTS

ACKNOWLEDGMENTS

I want to express my sincere gratitude to everyone who helped make this work possible by encouraging and supporting me. A special thank you to everyone who helped with our journey by kindly sharing their knowledge, offering insightful criticism, and providing constant encouragement. Your contributions have greatly enhanced this project.

CHAPTER 1

A COMPREHENSIVE GUIDE TO STRESS AND ANXIETY

1.1: The Stress Science

Stress Definition

The body's natural reaction to any demand or threat is stress. The "fight-or-flight" reaction, often referred to as the stress response, is the quick, instinctive process by which the body's defenses go into overdrive in the face of difficulty or danger. The purpose of this physiological response is to get the body ready to either face or run away from the perceived threat. Positive events and changes can also induce stress; negative experiences are not the only ones that can do so.

Stress Types

1. **Acute Stress:** The most prevalent kind of stress is

typically transient. The body's initial response to a novel demand, event, or challenge is known as acute stress. In moderation, it can be thrilling and exciting, but excessive acute stress can cause physical and psychological discomfort. An exam, a first date, or a job interview are a few instances of stressful situations.

2. **Chronic Stress:** Persistent and extended in nature, chronic stress differs from acute stress. It results from persistent circumstances that are hard to escape and feel unavoidable, including a demanding job, a problematic relationship, or money troubles. Prolonged stress can have detrimental effects on one's health, increasing the risk of diabetes, heart disease, and mental health issues.

3. **Episodic Acute Stress:** People who frequently encounter acute stress are susceptible to this kind of stress. Individuals who experience episodic acute stress are usually tense and anxious, feeling overburdened by all of the obligations and pressures in their lives. One could characterize them as

"constantly in crisis mode" or as having "a lot on their plate." Like chronic stress, this type of stress can cause ongoing emotional and physical discomfort.

The Stress-Reaction of the Body (Fight-or-Flight)

The brain's hypothalamus triggers the body's alarm system when it senses a threat. This system causes the adrenal glands, which are found atop the kidneys, to release a rush of hormones, such as cortisol and adrenaline, through a mix of nerve and hormonal impulses.

- **Adrenaline** raises blood pressure, quickens the heartbeat, and improves energy levels.
- The main stress hormone, **cortisol,** raises blood sugar (glucose) levels, improves how well your brain uses glucose, and increases the availability of nutrients that help heal damaged cells. It also disables processes that in a fight-or-flight scenario might be harmful or unnecessary.

Additionally, this intricate natural alarm system connects

with the brain's motivation, emotion, and fear centers. The stress response in the body is vital for survival because it enables people to react quickly to threats. On the other hand, persistent activation of this reaction can result in a number of health issues, emphasizing the significance of efficient stress management.

1.2: The Connection Between Anxiety and Stress

How Anxiety Is Triggered by Stress

Anxiety and stress are intimately associated; they frequently occur together and have an impact on one another. Stress is a reaction to an outside factor, such a pressing deadline at work or a contentious disagreement with a friend. Usually, as the issue is fixed, it goes away. Contrarily, anxiety is a person's unique response to stress and is typified by a lingering sense of unease or dread, even in the absence of the stressor.

Anxiety can be brought on by stress that becomes unbearable or persistent. This occurs because the body's stress response, which is intended to deal with immediate situations, is kept active for a long time. Prolonged release of stress hormones such as cortisol can alter brain chemistry and exacerbate anxiety. For instance, the hippocampus, a region of the brain involved in memory and emotional regulation, might shrink as a result of elevated cortisol levels, making anxiety management more challenging.

Anxiety's Effect on General Well-Being

Anxiety can significantly affect one's emotional and physical well-being. It can manifest physically as headaches, tense muscles, restless nights, and digestive problems. Additionally, long-term anxiety can impair immunity, leaving people more vulnerable to disease.

Anxiety can psychologically cause irritation, difficulty concentrating, and a persistent sensation of worry. These symptoms have the potential to seriously lower a person's quality of life over time by making it more difficult for them to go about their everyday lives, maintain relationships, and accomplish their personal and professional objectives.

Common Disorders of Anxiety

1. **Generalized Anxiety Disorder (GAD)**: Defined by excessive and ongoing concern over a range of life issues, including relationships with others, employment, and health. GAD sufferers struggle to stop worrying, which can cause disruptions to their everyday routines.

2. **Panic Disorder:** Consists of frequent, unprovoked episodes of great terror, sometimes accompanied by palpitations, perspiration, shaking, and a sense of imminent disaster. An ongoing fear of experiencing another panic attack is a common symptom of panic disorder and can have a serious negative influence on day-to-day functioning.

3. **Social Anxiety Disorder:** Characterized by a severe fear of social settings where one could be looked down upon, humiliated, or examined by others. Avoiding social situations can result from this illness, which can harm possibilities for both

personal and professional relationships.

1.3: Identifying Stress and Anxiety Symptoms

Physical Signs of Anxiety and Stress

For prompt diagnosis and management, it is essential to identify the bodily manifestations of stress and anxiety. Typical physical signs and symptoms include of:

- **Headaches:** Prolonged stress can cause tension headaches or migraines.
- **Muscle Tension:** Stress can lead to strained and aching muscles, particularly in the shoulders and neck.
- **Sleep Disturbances**: Anxiety and stress are frequently indicated by trouble falling or staying asleep or by restless sleep.
- **Digestive Issues:** Stress can cause symptoms such as diarrhea, constipation, or stomachaches by impairing digestion.
- **Fatigue:** A persistent sense of exhaustion and low energy can be brought on by long-term stress and

anxiety.

- **Increased Heart Rate:** Stress sets off the fight-or-flight reaction, which causes the heart to beat more quickly.

Feelings and Actions Indicative of Stress and Anxiety

Emotional and behavioral changes, such as the following, can also be signs of stress and anxiety:

- **irritation:** Stress can be indicated by elevated irritation and frustration, even over trivial matters.
- **Restlessness:** Anxiety and stress are frequently accompanied with a persistent sense of unease or an inability to unwind.
- **Difficulty Concentrating:** Anxiety and stress can affect cognitive abilities, making it difficult to concentrate or decide what to do.
- **Avoidance:** People may steer clear of circumstances or pursuits that they believe to be stressful or anxiety-provoking.
- **Changes in Eating Habits:** Stress can cause appetite fluctuations, resulting in an increase or

decrease in the amount of food consumed.

The Significance of Introspection

Effective stress and anxiety management begins with self-awareness. People can adopt coping mechanisms and take proactive steps to address the underlying reasons by identifying the symptoms and indicators. Frequent mindfulness and self-reflection exercises can improve self-awareness, enabling people to recognize stressors and comprehend their mental and physical reactions to them.

1.4: Gummies' Function in Stress Reduction

How Gummies Can Enhance Stress-Reduction Techniques

Gummies can be a useful supplement to stress-reduction plans, especially if they are made with natural components that are proven to have calming effects. They provide a practical and entertaining means of introducing stress-relieving substances into everyday existence. Gummies offer a diversified approach to lowering stress and anxiety because they can be used in conjunction with other stress-reduction techniques like physical activity, meditation, and good sleep hygiene.

The Advantages of Natural Gummy Ingredients

Numerous stress-relieving gummies are made with natural components that have been demonstrated to ease tension and encourage relaxation. Among these components are:

- **CBD (Cannabidiol):** Made from the hemp plant, CBD is well-known for relaxing the nervous system without having the same euphoric effects as THC.
- **Ashwagandha:** This adaptogenic herb fosters calmness and helps the body adjust to stress.
- **L-Theanine:** An amino acid present in green tea that helps people unwind without making them feel sleepy.
- **Melatonin:** An important hormone for stress management, it controls sleep-wake cycles and enhances the quality of sleep.
- **Chamomile:** A herb with calming qualities that is frequently used to ease anxiety and encourage sleep.

Selecting the Appropriate Gummies to Meet Your Needs

The precise contents and their intended effects should be taken into account while choosing gummies for stress relief. The following advice will help you select the ideal gummies:

- **Identify Your Needs:** Ascertain if you require assistance with reducing anxiety, relieving overall tension, or enhancing sleep.

- **Verify the Contents:** Seek for gummies with natural, premium components that have been shown to reduce tension and anxiety.

- **Read Reviews:** To determine the efficacy of the product, take into account user evaluations and testimonials.

- **Speak with a Medical Professional:** See your doctor to make sure a new supplement is safe and suitable for you before incorporating it into your regimen, particularly if you have underlying medical concerns or are on other drugs.

A person's general well-being can be greatly enhanced by learning about the science behind stress and its connection to anxiety, identifying the warning signs and symptoms, and investigating practical coping mechanisms like the use of gummies made of natural ingredients. Through proactive stress management, people can improve their quality of life and strengthen their ability to overcome obstacles.

INGREDIENTS' POWER

2.1: Adaptogens: The Natural Anti-Stress Agents

Definition of adaptogens:

Known for their capacity to support the body's resistance and adaptation to stress, adaptogens are a distinct class of herbs and other natural compounds. They function by providing support to the adrenal glands, which control the body's hormonal reaction to stress. Adaptogens, as opposed to conventional stimulants or sedatives, are non-specific and aid in balancing several physiological processes without having a noticeable negative impact. They support homeostasis by strengthening the body's resistance to chemical, biological, and physical stresses.

Well-liked Adaptogens for Reducing Stress

1. **Ashwagandha:** Known also as Withania somnifera, this age-old medicinal herb has been utilized for millennia in Ayurvedic medicine as a stress reliever. By lowering cortisol levels the hormone principally responsible for stress ashwagandha contributes to feelings of calmness and wellbeing. It also increases vigor and promotes mental wellness in general.

2. **Rhodiola:** The plant Rhodiola rosea is found in chilly, mountainous areas of Asia and Europe. It is well renowned for its capacity to strengthen the body's defenses against weariness and stress. In order to affect the levels and activities of neurotransmitters that are important for mood regulation, like dopamine and serotonin, rhodiola acts.

3. **Ginseng:** Panax quinquefolius, an American ginseng, and Panax ginseng, an Asian ginseng, are both well-known for their adaptogenic qualities. Through immune system support and adrenal gland regulation, ginseng helps to minimize the impacts of

stress, increase mental clarity, and boost physical performance.

How Adaptogens Reduce Anxiety and Stress

The primary stress response mechanism, the hypothalamic-pituitary-adrenal (HPA) axis, is modulated in part by adaptogens. Adaptogens lessen the overproduction of stress hormones like cortisol by improving the body's capacity to handle stress. This modulation contributes to the body's restoration of equilibrium, which raises mood, energy levels, and cognitive performance. Furthermore, adaptogens enhance general health and wellbeing by shielding cells from the damaging effects of long-term stress through their antioxidant qualities.

2.2: Nutrients That Elevate Mood

Minerals and Vitamins for Stress Reduction

1. **Vitamin B Complex:** An intact neurological system and proper brain function depend on the B vitamins, which include B1 (thiamine), B2 (riboflavin), B3

(niacin), B5 (pantothenic acid), B6 (pyridoxine), B7 (biotin), B9 (folate), and B12 (cobalamin). They are essential for the production of neurotransmitters, which control mood and stress reactions. Anxiety, despair, and irritability can all rise in response to B vitamin deficiencies.

2. **Magnesium:** The body uses magnesium to support more than 300 metabolic activities, including those that are related to stress reduction. It lessens cortisol release and aids in neurotransmitter regulation. A shortage in magnesium is frequently associated with elevated levels of stress, anxiety, and insomnia. Taking magnesium supplements can help with general mental wellness and relaxation.

3. **Zinc:** The health and cognitive function of the brain depend on zinc. In addition to supporting the immune system, it modulates the brain's reaction to stress. Zinc is a crucial mineral for mental health since it has been linked to fewer feelings of anxiety and depression when levels are adequate.

The Function of Fatty Acids Omega-3 in Reducing Stress

The brain requires omega-3 fatty acids, especially docosahexaenoic acid (DHA) and eicosapentaenoic acid (EPA). The brain contains large amounts of these polyunsaturated fats, which are necessary for healthy brain function. Inflammation can be decreased and neurotransmitter production regulated by omega-3 fatty acids, which can elevate mood and lessen anxiety and stress. Omega-3 supplements have been demonstrated in studies to improve general emotional resilience and reduce cortisol levels.

How These Nutrients Help Maintain Mental Health

These vitamins, minerals, and fatty acids work together to maintain the construction and function of the brain, control mood, and enhance the body's ability to handle stress. People can lessen their symptoms of anxiety and depression, improve their mental toughness, and preserve their general psychological well-being by making sure they are getting enough of these nutrients.

2.3: Natural Calming Herbs

Soothing Herbs

1. **Chamomile:** Known for its relaxing properties, chamomile is a popular herb. It has an antioxidant called apigenin, which attaches to specific brain receptors to induce calmness and lessen anxiety. A popular natural treatment for anxiety and sleep issues is chamomile tea.

2. **Lavender:** Lavender is well known for its calming scent and capacity to lessen tension and anxiety. Lavender's active ingredients, like linalyl acetate and linalool, have sedative and anxiolytic effects. To encourage relaxation, lavender oil can be taken orally as a supplement or utilized in aromatherapy.

3. **Valerian:** For millennia, people have utilized the root of Valerian to relieve anxiety and insomnia. It has substances that raise the brain's concentration of gamma-aminobutyric acid (GABA), such as

valerenic acid and valepotriates. One neurotransmitter that calms the nervous system is called GABA.

How Herbal Extracts Help Reduce Nervousness

Herbal extracts diminish the physiological and psychological symptoms of anxiety by promoting relaxation and interfering with the central nervous system. They have the power to affect neurotransmitter systems that control mood and stress reactions, like serotonin and GABA. These herbs' relaxing properties can lessen anxiety symptoms, promote better sleep, and improve general well being.

Safety Guidelines for Supplements Including Herbs

Although using herbal medicines to reduce stress and anxiety might be beneficial, it's crucial to utilize them carefully. The quality and concentration of active components in herbal medicines can differ greatly, and not all herbal products are made equal. It is necessary to:

- **Consult a Healthcare Professional:** To ensure safety and prevent potential interactions, see a healthcare practitioner prior to beginning any new herbal supplement, especially if you are taking other medications or have underlying medical issues.

- **Verify the Quality:** Select dietary supplements from reliable companies who offer independent third-party testing and product verification.

- **Adhere to Dosage Guidelines:** To prevent negative effects, follow the manufacturer's or your healthcare provider's suggested dosages and instructions.

2.4: The Science of Candy

How Gummies Effectively Deliver Nutrients

Dietary supplements in the form of gummies are widely used because they are sweet, easy to eat, and handy. By being chewed and broken down in the mouth, they efficiently supply nutrients and facilitate the release and absorption of the active substances. Certain minerals can also be made more bioavailable by the gelatin or pectin base of gummies, which makes it easier for the body to absorb them.

Aspects to Take Into Account While Selecting Gummy Supplements

The following elements should be taken into account while choosing gummy supplements:

1. Note the **Ingredients**: Look for gummies made entirely of natural, high-quality ingredients free of artificial flavors, colors, or preservatives. To make sure the supplement satisfies your unique needs, check the label for the active ingredients and their concentrations.

2. **Sugar Content:** To improve their flavor, many candies have sugar added to them. Pay attention to the amount of sugar, particularly if you are watching how much sugar you eat. There are brands that provide low-sugar or sugar-free solutions.

3. **Allergen Information:** Make sure the product is appropriate for your needs by looking for possible allergens if you have dietary restrictions or allergies.

4. **Brand Reputation:** Select dietary supplements from

respectable companies that have gained good consumer feedback and a certification for good manufacturing practices (GMP).

Quality and Purity Are Important

The quality and purity of gummy supplements have a major impact on their efficacy and safety. Premium gummies are free of impurities and manufactured with carefully chosen components. To be sure the product you are purchasing is secure and functional, check for:

- **Third-Party Testing:** Independent testing conducted by unbiased labs can confirm the supplement's quality, efficacy, and purity.
- **Transparency:** Reputable companies give thorough details regarding their sourcing, production methods, and quality assurance procedures.
- **Certifications:** Seek certifications that attest to adherence to strict quality standards, such as GMP, NSF, or USDA Organic.

Knowing the potential of components like adaptogens,

minerals that improve mood, and relaxing herbs can greatly improve stress management and general wellbeing. A fun and easy method to include these healthy nutrients in your everyday routine is using gummies. People can enhance their resilience to stress and preserve better mental health by choosing high-quality, efficient supplements and combining them with other stress management techniques.

CHAPTER 3

Gummies for Various Degrees of Anxiety

3.1: Stress and Mild Anxiety

Determining Symptoms of Mild Anxiety

Mild anxiety and stress are frequent reactions to a variety of real-world events, including social interactions, work pressures, and minor health issues. Mild anxiety symptoms include:

- Experiencing agitation or anxiety
- Moderate irritation
- Trouble focusing - Mild tenseness in the muscles
- Sleep issues

Early detection and appropriate management of these symptoms can prevent more severe types of anxiety from developing.

Mummy for Occasionally Worried and Stressed Out

Gummies made of natural substances can help people who are mildly anxious. Some common gummies are:

- **Lemon Balm:** Well-known for its relaxing properties, this balm can ease stress and elevate mood.
- **L-Theanine:** This amino acid, which is present in tea leaves, encourages relaxation without making you feel sleepy.
- **CBD (Cannabidiol):** Made from hemp, CBD is a non-psychoactive substance that has been demonstrated to ease anxiety and encourage serenity.

These components are good for those with mild anxiety symptoms since they can help reduce occasional stress and worry.

Modifications to Lifestyle to Balance Gummy Use

Apart than consuming gummies, implementing specific lifestyle modifications might also aid in the management of minor anxiety:

- **Regular Exercise:** Exercise raises endorphin production, which elevates mood and lowers stress.
- **Healthy Diet:** Eating a diet high in fruits, vegetables, and whole grains that is well-balanced can have a favorable effect on mental health.
- **Adequate Sleep:** Keeping up mental and emotional health requires getting enough sleep.
- **Mindfulness and Relaxation Techniques:** Activities like yoga, deep breathing exercises, and meditation can help lower anxiety and enhance mental health in general.

3.2: Mildly Concerned

Identifying Mild Anxiety

Compared to mild anxiety, moderate anxiety is more enduring and disruptive. Among the symptoms could be:

- Anxiety or panic that is difficult to regulate on a regular basis; conspicuous restlessness or tension; exhaustion; difficulty focusing; elevated heart rate; more severe sleep disruptions

Because these symptoms can impair one's quality of life and daily activities, management must take a more systematic approach.

Snacks to Handle Everyday Difficulties

The following mix of chemicals is commonly found in gummies designed for moderate anxiety:

- **Adaptogens (Rhodiola, Ashwagandha):** These herbs support the body's ability to stay balanced and adjust to stress.
- **Magnesium:** This mineral aids in the reduction of anxiety symptoms and strengthens the neurological system.
- **5-HTP (5-Hydroxytryptophan):** 5-HTP is a precursor to serotonin and has been shown to alleviate anxiety and elevate mood.

These candies offer a steady degree of anxiety alleviation and support in managing everyday obstacles.

Gummies in Combination with Relaxation Methods

When using gummies to treat mild anxiety, it can be helpful to combine their use with relaxing techniques to increase their effectiveness:

- **Progressive Muscle Relaxation (PMR):** To ease physical stress and anxiety, this technique entails tensing and then relaxing each muscle group.
- **Guided Imagery:** Focusing attention away from anxious thoughts can be achieved by imagining peaceful scenes or scenarios.
- **Biofeedback:** This technique, which uses electronics to track physiological processes, teaches people how to manage their stress reactions.

3.3: Extreme Fear

Comprehending Extreme Anxiety

Severe anxiety can appear as intense, ongoing fear or worry and severely hinders day-to-day functioning. Among the symptoms are:

- Episodes of panic
- Avoiding circumstances that make you anxious
- Severe physical symptoms (such as chest discomfort or shortness of breath) - Uncontrollably persistent concern - Profound disruption of social, academic, or occupational activities

Treatment for severe anxiety frequently needs to be all-encompassing.

Gummies as a Component of an All-Inclusive Therapy

Although gummies can help with acute anxiety, a more comprehensive treatment approach should include the following:

1. **Prescription Drugs:** These include benzodiazepines and selective serotonin reuptake inhibitors (SSRIs),

which are prescribed by medical professionals.

2. **Therapy:** When treating extreme anxiety, cognitive-behavioral therapy, or CBT, is especially helpful.

3. **Lifestyle Modifications:** These include consistent exercise, a balanced diet, and appropriate sleeping habits.

4. **Partnerships:** Making connections with like-minded people might offer coping mechanisms and emotional support.

The Significance of Expert Counseling

People who suffer from extreme anxiety should consult a professional. A medical professional may:

- **Diagnose the Condition:** Making sure the right treatment plan and diagnosis are determined.

- **Monitor Progress:** Modifying treatments as necessary to achieve the best results.

- **Offer Support:** Providing the person and their family with resources and assistance.

3.4: Gummies for Particular Types of Anxiety

Generalized Anxiety Disorder (GAD) Gummies

The hallmark of generalized anxiety disorder is excessive, unmanageable worry over a variety of everyday issues. Gummies that can aid in GAD management usually include:

- **CBD:** Promotes calmness and lessens anxiety.
- **Passionflower:** Well-known for its ability to soothe and lessen GAD symptoms.
- **Valerian Root:** Reduces anxiety and enhances quality of sleep.

These components have the potential to lessen the persistent anxiety linked to GAD.

Panic Disorder Gummies

Recurrent, unprovoked panic episodes and a dread of more attacks are symptoms of panic disorder. Some possible gummies for panic disorder are:

- **L-Theanine:** Encourages calmness and lessens the incidence of panic episodes.
- **Magnesium:** Promotes the health of the neurological system and helps shield against panic episodes.
- **Chamomile:** Has a relaxing effect that can assist in the treatment of severe anxiety.

These candies can help control general symptoms and offer immediate relief during panic attacks.

Social Anxiety Disorder Gummies

Extreme social anxiety disorder is characterized by a dread of being inspected or criticized by others in social circumstances. For this condition, gummies frequently include:

- **Rhodiola:** Enhances mood and lessens social anxiety.
- **Kava Kava:** renowned for its ability to soothe and lessen social anxiety.

- **Gamma-Aminobutyric Acid (GABA):** A neurotransmitter that aids in relaxation and anxiety reduction.

People who use these components may find it easier to relax in social settings.

Gummies can be a useful tool for controlling various anxiety levels. People can reduce anxiety and enhance their general well-being by selecting the appropriate formulation and combining the usage of gummies with other useful techniques. Always seek the advice of a healthcare expert to determine the best course of action for your unique circumstances.

CHAPTER 4

FORMULATING A COMPREHENSIVE STRATEGY

4.1: The Mind-Body Connection

How Stress Affects Physical Health

Although stress is a normal reaction to difficult circumstances, prolonged stress can be harmful to one's physical well-being. It is capable of

- **Weaken the immunological System:** Extended stress impairs immunological response, increasing susceptibility to diseases and infections.

- **Increase the Risk of Chronic Diseases:** Heart disease, hypertension, diabetes, and gastrointestinal problems are among the disorders that are made worse by stress.

- **Impact on Musculoskeletal Health**: Stress-related

tension can cause headaches and persistent muscle soreness.

- **Impact Hormonal Balance**: Prolonged stress can upset hormone balance, which can have an impact on reproductive health and metabolism.

The significance of appropriately managing stress is highlighted by the comprehension of its significant effects on the body.

Meditation and Mindfulness to Reduce Stress

Meditation and mindfulness are effective methods for lowering stress. They consist of:

1. **Mindfulness:** Mindfulness is the practice of being totally present in the moment, which breaks the pattern of negative thoughts that cause stress. careful breathing, body scans, and careful monitoring of thoughts and emotions are some of the techniques.

2. **Meditation:** By encouraging calmness and mental clarity, several types of meditation, including mantra meditation, loving-kindness meditation, and guided

imagery, help lower stress.

Regular application of these methods can increase emotional control, drastically lower stress levels, and improve general well being.

The Advantages of Physical Activity and Exercise

Engaging in physical activity is crucial for managing stress. Practice:

- **Reduces Stress Hormones:** The body's main stress hormone, cortisol, is lowered by physical activity.
- **Boosts Endorphins:** Exercise causes the brain's natural painkillers and mood enhancers, endorphins, to be produced at a higher rate.
- **Improves Sleep:** Frequent exercise helps control sleep cycles, which promotes greater rest and lower levels of stress.
- **Improves Cognitive Function**: Exercise helps mitigate the negative effects of stress by enhancing focus, memory, and general brain function.

Regular physical activity, such as jogging, yoga, strength training, or walking, can be very beneficial for stress management.

4.2: Stress Reduction and Diet

Dietary Influence on Stress and Anxiety

In order to effectively manage stress and anxiety, diet is essential. Certain nutrients have an impact on mental well-being and brain function. Bad eating habits, such as a lot of sugar and processed foods, can make the symptoms of anxiety and stress worse. On the other hand, a balanced diet promotes ideal bodily and mental well-being.

Dietary Items that Encourage Calm

Including particular items in your diet can aid in relaxation and stress reduction:

Complex carbohydrates (foods high in whole grains and legumes): Serotonin is a neurotransmitter that helps people feel peaceful.

- **Omega-3 Fatty Acids:** These fats, which are present in walnuts, flaxseeds, and seafood, lower inflammation and promote mental wellness.

- **Magnesium-Rich Foods:** Magnesium is found in nuts, seeds, and leafy greens, and it helps control cortisol levels.

- **Foods High in Antioxidants:** Vegetables, nuts, and berries help fight oxidative stress, which can exacerbate anxiety.

Selecting these items can assist in developing a diet that promotes stress reduction.

Developing a Nutritious and Balanced Diet

In order to properly manage stress with eating, strive for a well-balanced diet consisting of:

- **Vegetables and Fruits:** Packed with antioxidants, vitamins, and minerals, these foods promote general health and wellbeing.

- **Lean Proteins:** These include plant-based proteins, fish, and chicken. These foods supply the necessary amino acids needed to produce neurotransmitters.

- **Healthy Fats:** Fish, nuts, and seeds are good sources of omega-3 and omega-6 fatty acids, which are essential for brain function.

- **Whole Grains:** Boosting serotonin production and offering a consistent energy source.

Keeping up a diet rich in these foods can aid in stress reduction and improve general health.

4.3: Relieving Stress and Sleep

The Link Between Stress and Sleep

Stress and sleep are intimately associated. Stress can be exacerbated by sleep deprivation, and it can also make it difficult to fall and remain asleep. Prolonged sleep deprivation may cause:

1. **Impaired Cognitive Function:** Having an impact on judgment, focus, and memory.

2. **Mood Disturbances:** Resulting in depression, anxiety, and irritability.

3. **Weakened Immune System:** Increases susceptibility to diseases within the body.

4. **Increased Risk of Chronic Conditions**: These include cardiovascular illnesses, diabetes, and hypertension.

Getting a good night's sleep is crucial to stress management.

Hygiene Advice for Better Sleep

Enhancing sleep hygiene can lower stress and improve the quality of your sleep:

- **Create a Routine:** Even on the weekends, go to bed and wake up at the same time every day.

- **Establish a Calm Environment:** Make sure the bedroom is quiet, dark, and cold. Limit noise and make use of cozy bedding.

- **Reduce Screen Time:** To prevent blue light from disrupting the sleep cycle, turn off displays (computers, tablets, and phones) at least an hour before going to bed.

- **Avoid Stimulants:** Limit your intake of nicotine and caffeine, particularly at night.

- **Practice Relaxation Techniques:** Before going to bed, partake in peaceful activities like reading, taking a warm bath, doing moderate yoga, or practicing meditation.

Sweethearts for Better Sleep

Certain candies with substances like these can help improve the quality of your sleep:

- **Melatonin:** A hormone that helps to enhance the start and quality of sleep by controlling sleep-wake cycles.

- **Chamomile:** Well-known for its ability to induce peaceful sleep and calm down.

- **Valerian Root:** Promotes better sleep and lowers anxiety.

Incorporating these gummies into your nighttime routine will help you sleep better and feel less stressed.

4.4: Developing Hardiness

Creating Stress-Reduction Strategies

Creating efficient coping strategies to handle stress is a necessary part of building resilience:

1. **Cognitive Behavioral Techniques:** Distinguishing and substituting realistic, positive thought patterns for negative ones.
2. **Problem-Solving Skills:** The ability to deconstruct difficult circumstances into digestible chunks and come up with workable answers.
3. **Time Management:** To avoid burnout, prioritize your work, make reasonable goals, and take regular breaks.

The Significance of Social Assistance

Social support is essential for stress management and resilience building:

1. **Friends and Family:** Having a solid support system

can offer consolation on an emotional level, help when needed, and a feeling of inclusion.

2. **Support Groups:** Associating with others who have gone through comparable circumstances can provide insightful counsel, empathy, and motivation.

3. **Professional Assistance:** Consulting with therapists or counselors can offer organized assistance and useful coping mechanisms.

Developing an Upbeat Attitude

Resilience and stress management can be greatly impacted by a good mindset:

1. **Gratitude Practice:** Stress reduction and mood enhancement can result from consistently recognizing and valuing life's good elements.

2. **Optimism**: Resilience can be strengthened by keeping an optimistic outlook and concentrating on possible advantages.

3. **Self-Compassion:** Rather than being critical of oneself when under stress, practicing self-compassion can help one feel better emotionally.

By combining these techniques, people can improve their general quality of life and resilience in the face of adversity, as well as establish a holistic approach to stress management.

CHAPTER 5

GUMMIES TO MEET THE SPECIAL NEEDS OF WOMEN

5.1: Stress and Hormonal Influences

Hormones' Part in Women's Stress

Women's experiences with and responses to stress are greatly influenced by hormones. Important hormonal stages consist of:

1. **Menstrual Cycle:** Stress levels and mood can be affected by variations in progesterone and estrogen. Premenstrual syndrome (PMS) can make anxiety and stress worse for some women.

2. **Pregnancy and Postpartum:** Mood swings, anxiety, and stress can all be exacerbated by hormonal changes that occur both during and after pregnancy.

3. **Menopause:** Mood swings, anxiety, and elevated stress can be brought on by the decrease in estrogen during menopause.

Comprehending these hormonal impacts facilitates the creation of focused stress-reduction tactics.

Hormone Fluctuation Management Gummies

Gummies designed to treat hormone imbalances can lessen the effects of stress:

1. **Chasteberry**: Known to balance hormones and reduce PMS symptoms.
2. **Evening Primrose Oil**: Helps lessen mood swings and discomfort associated with menstruation.
3. **Dong Quai:** A plant that lowers menopausal symptoms and balances estrogen levels.

Gummies containing these components may offer a practical and efficient means of addressing hormonal stress.

Enhancing the General Well-Being of Women

Beyond regulating cyclical changes in hormones, maintaining general health is essential. Candies that consist of:

1. **Vitamins B6 and B12:** Crucial for controlling stress and mood.
2. **Magnesium:** Aids in tension relief and muscular relaxation.
3. **Adaptogens, such as Ashwagandha:** Assists the body in managing stress.

These nutrients support a comprehensive strategy for women's health that addresses both general and hormonal wellbeing.

5.2: Women's Health and Stress

The Effects of Stress on the Physical Health of Women

Prolonged stress can have significant negative impacts on women's physical health, such as:

1. **Cardiovascular Health:** Higher risk of hypertension and heart disease.

2. **Reproductive Health:** irregular menstrual periods, problems with conception, and pregnancy complications.

3. **Digestive Problems:** Irritable bowel syndrome (IBS) and other digestive diseases can be made worse by stress.

For the purpose of therapy and prevention, it is imperative to understand the connection between stress and physical health.

Gummies for Particular Health Issues with Women

Certain women's health conditions can be addressed by targeted gummies:

1. **Cranberry Extract:** Promotes infection prevention and urinary tract health.

2. **Vitamin D and Calcium:** Vital for strong bones, particularly during menopause.

3. **Probiotics:** Enhance digestive well-being and lessen

gastrointestinal symptoms brought on by stress.

These components support stress management and physical health maintenance.

Avoiding Illnesses Associated with Stress

The management of ailments connected to stress requires prevention. Chronic disease risk can be decreased by using a daily regimen of stress management techniques and supplements. This comprises:

1. **Daily Exercise:** Improves physical well-being and lowers stress.
2. **Well-Balanced Diet:** Promotes stress reduction and general wellbeing.
3. **Mindfulness Exercises:** Enhances mental well-being and aids with stress management.

5.3: Anxiety in Women

Typical Anxiety Problems for Women

Women frequently experience particular anxiety problems, like:

1. **Work-Life Balance:** Balancing roles in the home and at work.
2. **Social Expectations:** The pressure to live up to expectations and norms set by society.
3. **Health-Related Anxiety:** Worries about menopause, pregnancy, and reproductive health.

These difficulties may worsen anxiety and have an adverse effect on general wellbeing.

Gummies to Help Women Manage Their Anxiety

Gummies designed specifically to help women who are anxious may be helpful:

1. **L-Theanine:** Encourages calmness without making you feel sleepy.
2. **5-HTP (5-Hydroxytryptophan):** Promotes the synthesis of serotonin, elevating mood and lowering anxiety.

3. **Passionflower:** Well-known for its ability to soothe and lessen tension.

Women who take daily pills containing these components report better anxiety management.

Helping Women Get Rid of Anxiety

Giving women the tools they need to manage their anxiety includes:

1. **Education:** Disseminating knowledge on stress and anxiety reduction strategies.
2. **Support Groups:** Establishing networks in which women can exchange tactics and experiences.
3. **Professional Help:** Encouraging women to seek therapy or counseling as needed.

These methods can provide women a greater sense of control over their emotional well-being.

5.4: Women's Self-Care

Establishing a Self-Care Schedule

Having a disciplined self-care regimen is crucial for stress management. Important elements consist of:

1. **Regular Exercise:** Exercise elevates mood and lowers stress.
2. A diet high in fruits, vegetables, lean meats, and healthy fats promotes general health. This is known as **Balanced Nutrition.**
3. **Mindfulness Practices:** Methods that encourage calmness and relaxation include yoga, meditation, and deep breathing techniques.

Establishing a regular schedule can aid in stress management and enhance general wellbeing.

Women's Stress Management Techniques

Techniques for managing stress that work well include:

1. **Time Management:** To avoid overload, prioritize your duties and establish reasonable goals.

2. **Relaxation Techniques:** Techniques for lowering stress include gradual muscle relaxation and guided imagery.

3. **Hobbies and Interests**: Partaking in enjoyable and soothing hobbies.

These methods can aid women in managing stress more skillfully.

Creating a Robust Support Network

Having a solid support network is essential for managing stress. This comprises:

1. **Family and Friends:** Offering both practical and emotional support.

2. **Support Groups:** Making connections with people who have gone through comparable struggles.

3. **Professional Support**: Consulting life coaches, therapists, or counselors.

Creating a network of support can provide you the tools and motivation you need to handle stress.

Gummies can significantly improve women's health and well-being by addressing these particular needs and assisting them in efficiently managing stress, anxiety, and general health.

CHAPTER 6

Gummies for Particular Difficulties in Living

6.1: Workplace Stress

Controlling Stress at Work

Stress at work is a prevalent problem that can have an impact on one's physical and mental well-being. It can originate from a number of things, including stressful schedules, conflicting personalities, and heavy workloads. Among the techniques for handling stress at work are:

1. **Time Management:** Setting realistic deadlines, dividing projects into digestible chunks, and prioritizing tasks.
2. **Organization:** To increase productivity and lower stress, keep your workstation tidy and orderly.
3. **Professional Boundaries:** To avoid burnout, learn

when to say no and assign responsibilities to others.

People can lower their stress levels and manage their workload more effectively by putting these strategies into practice.

Snacks to Boost Productivity and Focus

Gummies made to increase concentration and productivity might be a useful tool for stress management at work. Important components frequently consist of:

1. **Ginseng:** renowned for enhancing mental clarity and vitality.
2. **B Vitamins:** Necessary for the synthesis of energy and mental acuity.
3. **L-Theanine:** Aids in concentration maintenance by promoting relaxation without sleepiness.

Together, these components increase productivity and focus while lowering stress levels related to work-related tasks.

Establishing a Harmonious Work-Life Accord

Reducing stress at work requires striking a healthy work-life balance. This includes:

1. **Setting Boundaries:** Clearly defining personal time and work hours.
2. **Taking Breaks:** Throughout the day, take little pauses to relax and refuel.
3. **Participating in Leisure Activities:** Having interests and hobbies outside of work as a way to decompress and rejuvenate.

A healthy balance between work and personal life lowers the risk of burnout and contributes to overall well being.

6.2: Relationship Stress

Managing Stress in Relationships

Relationships may be a major cause of stress, whether they are with a spouse, family, or friends. The following are some helpful coping mechanisms for relationship stress:

1. **Communication:** Discuss problems and settle disputes through direct and truthful communication.
2. **Empathy:** Perceiving and taking into account the viewpoint of another individual.
3. **Compromise:** Resolving conflicts in a way that both parties can live with.

Emotional well-being and stress reduction can be significantly enhanced by positive interpersonal dynamics.

Emotional Support Gummies

Emotionally supportive gummies can help reduce relationship stress. Some ingredients that are very advantageous are:

- **St. John's Wort:** renowned for improving mood.
- **Rhodiola Rosea:** Lowers anxiety and assists the body in adjusting to stress.
- **Omega-3 Fatty Acids:** Enhances mood and promotes brain health.

These components combined into gummies may offer a practical means of promoting resilience and emotional well-being in interpersonal relationships.

Creating Robust and Durable Connections

Developing solid connections entails:

1. **Respect and Trust:** Essential components of any happy partnership.
2. **Quality Time:** Investing significant time in one another to fortify relationships.
3. **Supportive Networks:** Having a network of relatives and friends who can help you through trying times.

Relationships that are robust and strong can withstand stress and disagreement better, which improves general well being.

6.3: Parenting and Stress

Managing Stress in Parenting

Being a parent is a wonderful and demanding job that may cause a great deal of stress. Among the coping mechanisms for parenting stress are:

1. **Structure and Routine:** Creating patterns to foster stability and predictability.
2. **Self-Care:** Putting one's health first in order to stay patient and energetic.
3. **Support Systems:** Asking friends, family, and parenting organizations for assistance.

Parents who use effective coping mechanisms can reduce stress and get greater enjoyment out of becoming parents.

Snacks for the Welfare of Parents

Gummies designed with parents' health in mind might offer vital assistance. Ingredients that are beneficial include:

1. **Ashwagandha:** Assists in lowering tension and anxiety.
2. **Magnesium:** Promotes muscular function and

relaxation.

3. **Valerian Root:** Encourages higher caliber rest.

In spite of the challenges of parenting, these substances can aid parents in stress management and maintaining their wellbeing.

Putting Self-Care First

In order to effectively handle stress, parents must practice self-care. This comprises:

1. **Physical Activity:** Engaging in regular physical activity to improve mood and vigor.
2. **Balanced Nutrition:** Maintaining general health with a nutritious diet.
3. **Relaxation Techniques:** Stress-reduction methods like deep breathing exercises and meditation.

Making self-care a priority keeps parents healthy and better able to manage the demands of parenthood.

6.4: Teachers and Stress

Handling Stress in the Classroom

Exams, homework, and the pressure to achieve excellent marks are just a few of the academic stresses that cause major stress for students. Among the practical methods for reducing academic stress are:

1. **Time Management:** Planning your studies and establishing reasonable objectives.
2. **Study Techniques:** Making use of efficient study strategies like spaced repetition and active recall.
3. **Recess and Recreation:** In order to avoid burnout, schedule regular pauses and partake in recreational pursuits.

Students can lessen their stress and manage their workload by using these techniques.

Gummies to Boost Memory and Concentration

Students can benefit from gummies that are intended to

enhance memory and concentration in their academic pursuits. Important components consist of:

1. **Ginkgo Biloba:** Promotes memory and cognitive function.
2. **Bacopa Monnieri:** Well-known for enhancing concentration and learning.
3. **Lion's Mane Mushroom:** Promotes cognitive function and brain health.

These components can be added to gummies to give youngsters the mental support they require to succeed academically.

Developing Self-Assurance and Adaptability

Students need to develop resilience and self-assurance in order to tackle academic problems. This includes:

1. **Positive mentality:** Fostering a growth mentality in order to see obstacles as chances to learn.
2. **Supportive Environment:** Establishing a welcoming and upbeat atmosphere for learning.

3. **Stress-Management Strategies:** Using methods like deep breathing and mindfulness to help you relax.

By honing these abilities, students can become more resilient, manage stress well, and succeed academically.

Through focused tactics and supporting gummies, people can effectively manage stress and preserve overall well-being in multiple facets of their lives by tackling specific lifestyle difficulties.

CHAPTER 7

SLEEP AND GUMMIES

7.1: The Value of Rest

Slumber's Function in Stress Reduction

Sleep is essential for maintaining general health and wellbeing, especially when it comes to stress management. The body heals itself as we sleep, while the brain works through memories and emotions. A healthy immune system, improved cognitive performance, and mood regulation are all aided by getting enough sleep. Sleep is a natural defense against stress and anxiety because people who receive enough sleep are better able to face life's stresses.

The Effect of Lack of Sleep on Anxiety

Lack of sleep can have detrimental effects on mental health, aggravating anxiety among other things. Anxiety levels may rise as a result of increased synthesis of stress hormones like cortisol while sleep deprived. Chronic sleep loss can worsen cognitive abilities like focus, decision-making, and reaction time, which can increase stress and anxiety levels. Thus, getting enough good sleep is essential to effectively managing anxiety.

Creating a Sleep-Friendly Space

Having a sleep-friendly atmosphere is crucial to getting a good night's sleep. Important things to think about are as follows:

1. **Comfortable Bedding:** To promote restful sleep, spend money on a quality mattress and pillows.
2. **Darkness**: Blocking off light with an eye mask or blackout curtains.
3. **Noise Control:** Using a white noise machine or

earplugs to reduce noise.

4. **Temperature:** Maintaining a cool, well-ventilated bedroom.

People can increase their chances of obtaining restorative sleep, which in turn aids in the management of stress and anxiety, by making improvements to the sleep environment.

7.2: Gummies to Promote Better Sleep

Gummies have the potential to be a useful supplement for improving sleep quality. They frequently include organic components proven to promote healthy sleep, like:

1. **Melatonin:** A hormone that helps induce sleep by controlling the circadian rhythm.
2. **Chamomile:** A soothing plant that helps ease anxiety and encourage rest.
3. **Valerian Root:** renowned for its sedative qualities, which aid in enhancing the quality of sleep.

Together, these components facilitate a quicker transition

to sleep as well as deeper, more restorative slumber.

Selecting the Appropriate Gummies for Sleep

When choosing gummies to help you fall asleep, it's crucial to take things like:

1. **Ingredient Quality:** Verify that the gummies are made with natural, premium ingredients.
2. **Dosage:** To prevent any negative effects, take the prescribed amount as directed.
3. **Purity:** Seek for goods devoid of synthetic preservatives and additives.

Selecting the best sleep gummies can have a big impact on stress management and sleep quality.

7.3: Tips for Proper Sleep

Sleep hygiene refers to routines and behaviors that support regular, undisturbed sleep. Important guidelines for good sleep hygiene consist of:

1. **Regular Sleep Schedule:** Establishing a regular bedtime and wake-up time each day, including on the weekends.
2. **Pre-Sleep Routine:** Create a relaxing ritual before going to bed, like reading or having a warm bath.
3. **Reducing Screen Time:** To lessen exposure to blue light, turn off electronics at least one hour before bed.
4. **Avoiding Stimulants:** Refraining from caffeine and nicotine in the evenings because they have the potential to interfere with sleep.

Making use of these suggestions can assist in establishing a setting that is favorable for improved sleep and general wellbeing.

7.4: Solving Sleep Issues

Determining Sleep Issues

Insomnia, sleep apnea, restless legs syndrome, and night terrors are examples of common sleep disorders. Finding a workable solution starts with identifying the precise problem. Watch out for symptoms like fatigue when you wake up from sleep, trouble falling asleep, and frequent nighttime awakenings.

Taking Care of Sleep Issues

Often, treating sleep disorders calls for a diversified strategy:

1. **Medical Evaluation**: Speaking with a medical expert to determine any underlying issues.
2. **Behavioral Therapy:** Chronic sleep disorders can be effectively treated with cognitive-behavioral therapy for insomnia (CBT-I).
3. **Lifestyle Modifications:** Including stress-reduction strategies, a balanced diet, and frequent exercise in everyday routines.

Gummies as an Adjunctive Strategy

Gummies can be used as a component of a complete plan to address sleep issues. Melatonin and valerian root are two examples of ingredients that can help control sleep cycles and enhance the quality of sleep. But it's crucial to utilize these supplements under a doctor's supervision, particularly if you have serious sleep difficulties.

People can dramatically increase the quality of their sleep, lower stress levels, and improve their general health by combining gummies with appropriate sleep hygiene measures and treating any underlying sleep issues.

CHAPTER 8

8.1: Gaining Weight Due to Stress

The Link Between Stress and Gaining Weight

Stress has a major negative influence on weight control and frequently results in weight increase. People's bodies release the hormone cortisol in response to stress, which can enhance appetite and lead to desires for high-calorie foods. This physiological reaction has its origins in human evolutionary history, when stress was frequently interpreted as a signal for the need for quick energy, which resulted in a desire for meals high in calories.

Stress and Emotional Eating

Emotional eating is the term for the practice of many

people resorting to food as a comfort when they are under stress. This may result in consuming too many calories, especially from fatty and sugary foods, which can cause weight gain. In order to assuage unpleasant feelings rather than satiate physical hunger, emotional eating frequently ignores hunger indicators.

Persistent Stress's Effect on Metabolism

Metabolism can also be impacted by ongoing stress. Extended periods of stress can slow down metabolic functions, which makes it more difficult for the body to burn calories effectively. Stress can also cause sleep disturbances, which can result in further hormone imbalances that impact weight, like elevated ghrelin (hunger hormone) and decreased leptin (satiety hormone).

8.2: Gummies to Regulate Your Appetite

Gummies' Function in Controlling Appetite

Gummies made to suppress hunger can be a useful tool in managing weight. These candies frequently have components that support satiety and control appetite. Important components consist of:

1. **Garcinia Cambogia:** The hydroxycitric acid (HCA) in this tropical fruit extract is thought to reduce hunger by raising serotonin levels in the brain.

2. **Glucomannan:** A naturally occurring fiber that helps lower total calorie consumption by expanding in the stomach and promoting feelings of fullness.

3. **Chromium Picolinate:** This mineral can help manage appetite and lower sugar cravings by regulating blood sugar levels.

Achievement and Utilization

As recommended by the product label, hunger control gummies should be used before meals for best effects. These gummies must be used in conjunction with a nutritious diet and frequent exercise in order to promote and sustain weight loss.

8.3: Energy-Boosting Gummies

The Significance of Energy in Weight Control

Sustaining energy levels is essential for managing weight. Fatigue might make it harder to be motivated to exercise, which can result in a sedentary lifestyle and weight increase. On the other hand, a high energy level can improve activity levels and exercise performance, which can help burn calories and promote weight loss.

Components of Gummies That Boost Energy

Vitamins and natural stimulants are frequently used in energy-boosting candies to increase energy levels. Important components consist of:

1. **Caffeine:** A popular stimulant that can boost vitality and alertness. Moreover, it can increase metabolic rate, which promotes weight loss.

2. **Vitamin B Complex:** B vitamins are necessary for the body to turn food into energy and can help

sustain high energy levels all day.

3. **Green Tea Extract:** This blend of antioxidants, including EGCG, and caffeine can improve energy and metabolism of fat.

Energy and Appetite Balance

Energy-boosting gummies can raise physical activity levels, but in order to avoid overindulging, it's crucial to balance their use with techniques for controlling appetite. To optimize these gummies' weight-management effects, pair them with a regimented exercise schedule.

8.4: Incorporating Healthy Habits with Gummies

Using Gummies to Adopt a Healthier Lifestyle

Gummies should be utilized as a component of a comprehensive strategy that includes stress management, regular exercise, and a nutritious diet in order to achieve long-term weight management. Important tactics consist of:

1. **Well-Balanced Diet:** Give priority to whole foods including fruits, vegetables, whole grains, and lean meats. Steer clear of processed foods that are heavy in sugar and bad fats.

2. **Regular Exercise:** To enhance general fitness and aid in weight loss, combine cardiovascular, strength, and flexibility activities.

3. **Mindful Eating:** To prevent overeating, employ mindful eating strategies including savoring each meal, eating deliberately, and paying attention to hunger cues.

Human Hydration's Role

Maintaining hydration is crucial for controlling weight. Enough water consumption can enhance metabolism, reduce appetite, and promote general health. To maximize their efficiency and ease of digestion, gummies should be consumed with lots of water.

Strategies for Stress Management

Using stress management techniques is essential because

there is a strong correlation between stress and weight gain. Deep breathing techniques, yoga, and mindfulness meditation are a few practices that can help lower stress levels and stop stress-related weight gain.

Tracing Development

Individuals can maintain motivation and make the required changes to their weight management plan by routinely monitoring their progress. This includes maintaining a food and exercise record, tracking weight, and taking measurements of the body.

Gummies' specific health benefits when combined with these wholesome living practices help people improve their efforts at managing their weight, reach their objectives, and sustain long-term success.

CHAPTER 9

ADVERSE REACTIONS AND SAFETY

9.1: Comprehending Substances

Importance of Understanding Ingredients

Comprehending the contents of dietary supplements is essential to guaranteeing their safety and effectiveness. Every element in a gummy supplement plays a distinct role and has several potential effects on the body. Users can avoid potential side effects and make informed decisions by being aware of these components.

Gummies' Common Ingredients

1. **Minerals and Vitamins:** These are vital elements that promote general well-being. Zinc, calcium, B vitamins, vitamin C, and vitamin D are typical

examples. Overindulgence might result in toxicity even while it is healthy.

2. **Herbal Extracts:** Due to their relaxing and stress-relieving qualities, ingredients such as ashwagandha, valerian root, and chamomile are frequently employed. To prevent contamination, it's critical to know their source and level of purity.

3. **Amino Acids:** Some gummies contain amino acids like tryptophan and L-theanine, which are believed to aid with sleep and relaxation.

4. **Sweeteners and Flavors:** To improve flavor, artificial or natural sweeteners and flavors are added. Some people can be allergic to certain substances or have sensitivity to them.

Researching and Reading Labels

Understanding the function and possible effects of the gummies can be aided by carefully reading labels and investigating each ingredient. To guarantee quality and safety, look for products with transparent labeling and independent testing.

9.2: Possible Adverse Reactions

Regular Adverse Effects

Even though gummies are usually thought to be safe, some people may have adverse consequences. Typical adverse effects consist of:

1. **Digestive Issues:** Some people may experience gas, bloating, or diarrhea from ingredients like fiber or specific plant extracts.

2. **Allergic Reactions:** Rashes, itching, swelling, and other allergic reactions may be brought on by some components.

3. **Overconsumption Risks:** Toxic effects may result from consuming too much vitamin and mineral content. For instance, an excess of iron might result in gastrointestinal irritation, and an excess of vitamin A can harm the liver.

Identifying Signs

Early detection of any side effect symptoms is crucial. It's important to stop using the product and get medical help if you're experiencing severe or ongoing negative effects.

9.3: Medication Interactions

Comprehending Communication

Gummies include certain chemicals that may interact with drugs to change their effectiveness or cause unfavorable effects. This is especially crucial for people on prescription drugs or those who have underlying medical issues.

Regular Exchanges

1. **Blood Thinners:** Certain ingredients, such as omega-3 fatty acids and vitamin K, may interfere with the effectiveness of blood-thinning drugs.
2. **Sedatives:** The effects of sedatives can be amplified by herbal extracts, such as melatonin and valerian root, which might result in excessive sleepiness.

3. **Diabetes drugs:** Certain herbs or minerals that influence blood sugar levels may interact with diabetes drugs, necessitating dosage modifications.

Value of Transparency

To prevent negative interactions, always let healthcare practitioners know about any supplements you're taking. This guarantees that when managing medications, all facets of health are taken into account.

9.4: Seeking Advice from a Medical Expert

The Significance of Consultation

Consulting a healthcare provider is crucial prior to beginning any new supplement program. This makes it easier to guarantee that the supplement is secure and suitable for the person's particular medical requirements and circumstances.

Advantages of Expert Advice

1. **Personalized Advice:** Medical experts can offer tailored guidance depending on a patient's medical background, ongoing prescriptions, and general state of health.

2. **Monitoring and Adjustment:** Routine examinations make it possible to keep an eye on the effects of the supplement and alter the dosage or kind as needed.

3. **Prevention of Adverse Effects:** Experts can assist in identifying any dangers and adverse effects, guaranteeing a safer supplementation regimen.

Selecting the Appropriate Expert

Seeking guidance from a qualified healthcare professional, such as a registered dietitian, pharmacist, or doctor, guarantees that the recommendations are reliable and supported by data. Refrain from making judgments about your health based only on the advice of unqualified people or internet resources.

People can safely include gummies to their wellness routine by knowing the components, identifying possible adverse effects, being aware of medication combinations, and speaking with healthcare specialists. This all-encompassing strategy guarantees that the advantages of gummies are optimized while lowering hazards.

CHAPTER 10

Health in the Long Run

10.1: Developing Hardiness

A Knowledge of Resilience

The capacity to adjust and recover from hardship, stress, and obstacles is known as resilience. It entails creating coping strategies and retaining mental toughness amid trying circumstances.

Methods for Developing Resilience

1. **Developing Positive Thinking:** Have a positive mindset and concentrate on possibilities and strengths rather than flaws and dangers.

2. **Embracing Change:** Acquire the ability to adjust to

obstacles and changes while seeing them as chances for personal development.

3. **Creating Sturdy Connections:** Encourage dependable bonds with loved ones and neighbors. Having social support is essential when under stress.

4. **Practicing Self-care:** Give self-care tasks that advance mental, emotional, and physical health top priority. This involves getting enough rest, working out frequently, and maintaining a balanced diet.

5. **Setting Realistic Goals:** Divide more ambitious objectives into more manageable tasks. Celebrate your accomplishments to keep the momentum and drive going.

10.2: Keeping Up a Healthful Way of Life

The Significance of Lifestyle Decisions

Maintaining a healthy lifestyle is essential for long-term well-being since it impacts mental and physical health as well as general quality of life.

Elements of a Well-Being Lifestyle

1. **Nutritious Diet:** Eat a well-balanced diet high in whole grains, fruits, vegetables, and lean meats. Reduce your consumption of sugar, processed foods, and saturated fats.

2. **Regular Exercise:** Exercise on a regular basis to enhance mood-enhancing endorphins, maintain a healthy weight, and promote cardiovascular health.

3. **Adequate Sleep:** Make good sleep hygiene a priority to guarantee restful sleep. Inadequate sleep can negatively impact mood stability, mental clarity, and general wellness.

4. **Stress Management:** To improve resilience and lower the risk of chronic diseases, engage in stress-reduction practices including mindfulness, deep breathing exercises, and meditation.

5. **Avoiding Harmful Substances:** To prevent harm to one's physical or mental health, cut back on alcohol intake and abstain from smoking and using illegal substances.

10.3: Getting Expert Assistance

When to Get Expert Assistance

It's critical to realize when more help from medical specialists is required to manage complex issues or mental health difficulties.

Significance of Seeking Assistance

Persistent Symptoms: In spite of self-help attempts, symptoms of anxiety, depression, or other mental health conditions continue.

Impact on Daily Life: Difficulties adjusting to emotional or psychological distress at work, school, or in relationships.

Suicidal Thoughts: Suicidal or self-harming thoughts must always be treated seriously and necessitate prompt medical attention.

Categories of Expert Assistance

1. **Therapy:** To encourage positive change, people can explore their thoughts, feelings, and behaviors with the assistance of cognitive-behavioral therapy (CBT), psychotherapy, or counseling sessions.

2. **Medication:** When used appropriately and under supervision, psychiatric drugs recommended by medical professionals help lessen the symptoms of mental health conditions.

3. **Support Groups:** Community services or peer support groups offer chances to interact with people going through comparable struggles and get emotional support.

10.4: A More Hopeful Tomorrow

Determining Objectives for Extended Well-being

1. **Personal Growth**: Constantly work toward your own personal development by picking up new skills, engaging in interests, and establishing worthwhile objectives.

2. **Career and Financial Stability:** Having a secure job and finances helps people feel better overall and less stressed.

3. **Healthy Relationships:** Foster wholesome bonds of respect, trust, and support with your family, friends, and lovers.

4. **Community Contribution:** To make a positive impact on society and develop a feeling of purpose, take part in volunteer work or community projects.

Retaining Health Throughout Time

Being self-aware, flexible, and dedicated to healthy behaviors are all necessary for long-term well-being. People can cultivate long-lasting well-being and lead happy lives by putting resilience first, leading healthy lifestyles, getting professional support when necessary, and making objectives for a better future.

ABOUT THE AUTHOR

Harmony Royce is a dedicated healthcare worker who has a strong interest in holistic wellness. Harmony's extensive history in various aspects of health and wellness provides her with a wealth of knowledge and expertise that she can utilize in her writing and professional endeavors.

Harmony is a talented author who crafts thought-provoking books that inspire readers to have well-rounded, balanced lives. She writes about a variety of health-related topics, such as diet, exercise, mental health, and mindfulness. Her approachable writing style combines practical guidance with evidence-based research to make complex health concepts approachable and engaging for readers of all ages.

Harmony actively promotes the benefits of holistic health through writing, community workshops, and internet forums. Her mission is to educate and inspire people about the transformative power of self-care and healthy lifestyle choices.

* 9 7 9 8 3 3 3 3 8 8 3 9 1 *